POETRY BIRMINGHAM

POETRY BIRMINGHAM
Literary Journal

Summer 2020 — Issue Four

EDITOR

Naush Sabah

PALLINA PRESS LIMITED.
BIRMINGHAM

POETRY BIRMINGHAM
Literary Journal

Pallina Press Limited, Birmingham
www.pallinapress.com

© 2020 all individual authors
All rights reserved. Published 2020

Typeset & Design: Suna Afshan, Adrian B. Earle, and Naush Sabah
Co-editor: Suna Afshan

ISSN 2633-0822
ISBN 9798642492048

COVER IMAGES

Wey, 1882-83
By William Morris
Watercolour for Printed Fabric Design
Photo by Birmingham Museums Trust, licensed under Creative Commons CC0

Wey furnishing fabric, 1883.
By William Morris
Block-printed cotton.
© Victoria and Albert Museum, London.

Birmingham
Museums

SUBMISSIONS

For our guidelines, visit www.poetrybirmingham.com

Submission windows:
1st to 30th June
1st to 31st October
1st to 28th February

The saviours come not home to-night:
  Themselves they could not save.

'1887', *A Shropshire Lad*, A. E. Houseman

the shadow long in front of her is her
vision, and she pursues it—or rather
it pulls her body along the dirt road:
an animal plodding, tied to its load.

'trip to yarl's wood', *heft*, Doyali Islam

'A time to sicken and to swoon,
    When Science reaches forth her arms
    To feel from world to world, and charms
Her secret from the latest moon?'

'In Memoriam A. H. H.', Alfred Lord Tennyson

Contents

EDITORIAL

Naush Sabah

Dis/rupt/ed Schemas

We are not living through unprecedented times

and that is no comfort.

❀

There's something ineffable at the heart of an effective poem. For all our theorising and analysis of craft and technique, there's something beyond articulation about how a certain poem manages to work upon the reader as it does. Or rather, something that is only, and *can only* be, articulated in the body and sound of the poem itself.

Post-proof: I realise the marginalia and main text are slightly at odds & am fine with that. We can live with & mull over countervailing contentions.

There's nothing ineffable about why other poems we come across, shared enthusiastically by prize-winning poets on social media for instance, are sent straight to DM to be eviscerated. How do I not rate it? Let me count the ways.

❀

Last March, I walked past Bassano's *St. Roch Visits the Plague-Stricken*. It made no impression upon me that I can recall. Most multitudes in misery, we can stroll or scroll by. What made the strongest impression were Hayez's *The Kiss* and Maineri's *Head of St. John The Baptist*. Individual grief or loss is singular. A poem's specificity is where the ineffable lies.

❀

15

I stopped to sit at a long bench in front of *St. Mark Preaching in Alexandria*, a huge Orientalist oil painting that occupies a gallery's entire wall. I took my backpack off and placed it beside me, and perhaps it touched the backpack of the man sitting next to me—though it was imperceptible and certainly didn't displace it—because he huffed loudly, snatching up his bag and removing it from the bench. Yes, by the way, of course he was. We sat in front of this imposing Orientalist masterpiece of a fictionalised ancient scene that pre-dates Islam but nonetheless depicts completely veiled Muslim women seated on the ground and surrounded by robed men. The Egyptian city in the painting is populated by Muslims in Turkish attire, interchangeable as the Others are to the Orientalist eye.

'Directive', Robert Frost

❀

I'm not one for turning the other cheek when made to feel unwelcome in public places. I often attempt to return the feeling of discomfort by at least naming it. 'This man is making *quite* the display of moving his bag away from me, perhaps my presence has annoyed him,' I said aloud, and he glared at me from behind his spectacles. I smiled and admired the giraffe in the painting. I like the painting. The giraffe and camels look fairly accurate.

❀

I wonder what it is about the Muslim women—sitting indistinguishable from one another at the feet of St. Mark—in the imagination of the Orientalist painter, that bears thoughtful, reverent, consideration in an art gallery.

I wonder what it is about the Muslim woman sitting in that gallery and gazing upon the painting that warrants physical and verbal signals of being unwelcome and held in contempt.

❀

People are dying. And we will talk about race. 'Why do you have to make everything about race?' Who gets to decide when to make things about race?

❀

Flaubert, in a letter to his Occidental mistress, whilst doing the most to get STDs on his travels through the Orient:

> The Oriental woman is a machine, and nothing more. She doesn't differentiate between one man and another. Smoking, going to the baths, painting her eyelids and drinking coffee, such is the circle of occupations which make up her existence. As for physical pleasure, it must be very slight since they cut off that famous button, the very place of it, quite early on. And for me, this is what renders this woman so poetic, that she becomes absolutely one with nature.

The Oriental woman might flick her cigarette at a man's feet. She might do very well with her button. She might be a poet who seeks pleasure making her way through Paris—managing to avoid syphilis—and writes assurances to her lover that the Occidental man can by no means be called a *machine*.

❀

At the beginning of March, I saw video footage of the Greek coast guard ramming and shooting at a dinghy full of refugees. In the middle of April, two refugees were shot in Greece during lockdown.

❀

'Ashglory', Paul Celan

No one bears witness for the witness.

We are still leaving the EU.

It's immigration, stupid.

Post-proof: Shall I replace this headline with a newer, even more grim one about the increased risk of death by race?

'BAME people make up 72% of all NHS and carer deaths with COVID-19'.

Adrian: melanin is *a comorbidity in a white nationalist society.*

Witness begets witness.

Carolyn Forché

❀

'BAME' people are tired and hate the acronym BAME. How many different ways can we say 'not white' without saying it and without saying who we actually are and who others are in relation to us?

❀

I should probably quote a poet or critic here. Why not Eliot? 'This is the wasteland,' she said as we drove through Stratford Road in Sparkbrook. 'This is where I grew up,' I replied. 'What are the roots that clutch, what branches grow / Out of this stony rubbish?'

❀

The libraries are closed. Google isn't enough. What do I work with now and where? On Twitter, writers are showing their shelves. I am seeing complete collections of Picador and Penguin and wondering what it must be like to have the wealth to accumulate and house such personal libraries. Here is the colour chart spread ceiling to floor, wall to wall in spines. Here are our novelists, our editors, our creative writing lecturers. Here is what they are working with.

❀

I am wondering what it must be like to have enough time at your disposal to read that many books, to write that many books; to not scrape out the moments between survival, domestic drudgery, and endless caregiving for what dried tubers of creativity or criticism you can grow out of your stony rubbish.

Post-proof: I wish I had the space to expound on this bit, to tell our readers how much this feels like pulling a rabbit out of a hat; cooking with thin air, like the meme.

Heaney, on what lies at the heart of a memorable reading: '. . . there is a sensation both of arrival and of prospect, so that one does indeed seem to 'recover a past' and 'prefigure a future'. . .'

Sparkbrook. 'Here there is no water but only rock / Rock and no water and the sandy road'. 'If there were water we should stop and drink / Amongst the rock one cannot stop or think'.

❁

. . . it evoked itself: rock, water, forest, settlers, trade. Then property sewage, architects, poets.'
'Six Texts for a Film', Roy Fisher

Lockdown is not an equal opportunities event. Life is not an equal opportunities event. We are not all in anything together. These things are not the same: a child who attends a private school now being educated by middle-class parents on furlough in Harborne; a child who attends a failing academy in Sparkbrook, now at home all day in a household where parents are low-paid key workers and siblings take on care duties. Extend the comparison to our poetry publications and editors, to our poets and critics, to our bookshelves and libraries, to our awards and prizes, to our judges and panels.

❁

Post-proof: 'Something about the cleaner discourse here?' :'No, I've read quite enough of that.'

I am looking at the Creative Case for Diversity on the ACE website. I am looking at the Executive Board of ACE on the ACE website. I am looking at the Creative Case for Diversity on the ACE website. I am looking at the names and face and biographies of the Executive Board of ACE on the ACE website. I am tabbing back and forth between the two on my browser.

❁

David Holbrook, in 1980: '. . . given an Arts Council . . . and bureaucracies — can we really hope for State funds for real art, to support the intransigent agonies of a genuine engagement with Being?'

I am looking at the 'diversity' of poetry publishing and seeing melanated variations of the same strata of society from different points of origin around the world. I am seeing the melting pot that is Oxbridge. I am looking at publishers' lists and seeing Oxbridge colleges, Instagram/ Twitter follower numbers, adopted performative identities and their branding.

❁

I am looking at the mirror, looking at our pages.

❁

Everything has been disrupted. Ruptured. Rent. This is not what things are supposed to look like. This is not what an editorial is supposed to look like, sound like, how it's supposed to be shaped. But how else do we mark the change to our rhythms and rituals than by changing our rhythms and rituals?

❁

Still, in the end, very little has changed.

Khaled Hakim

Three Walking Poems

Howsholder

    I, a routene dat carriz a child until asleep
it wawks owt of libraryz & anonymus scools in serch of sumething nearer than
a park
    it walks in a lust of words, waere the anger for words remoovs to modulated
anger
    dere is a hunger of the elefant in the universiti

    da waiht of my child on a page
    how much doz it waiy—how much da waiʒt of a cild in Inglish—da waiyt
of further educashun
    now add da faðerz cramping arms, now add a father as an moðer, a father
trudjing lybrary scool & park—a man who dozent kno if hees wawking a babby
to see th ducks or wawking down his yers
    add a luckless father w/ a radiant baby looking at wolvz on a leesh &
Japaneze fihting dogs & geese
    now add þe goldfish to mock medievel mote
    & green water churning columms of slurry
    how much doz a baby waih on a middelaged page—can yu wayʒ my cild
in middel English? can y/ carry a cild
    heere

    Wats he looking at?
    Yoo ar Emptiness looking thruʒ a cild holding him by th hand
    put it down on a page—
    yuve got th words—now carry him
    hwats a parent doing carrying his cild? do yoo hav children? Well, go on ye
gimp—carry yer own dad
    can y/ feel how hevvy he wayz in proze? Can y/ feel how hevvy he wayz
in poetri?
    Then hwat is poetri?
    Ðer is an silenss in a semi open kicchen & a radianss arownd an unseen
clock, & th muffeld muzick behind unnown walls
    ane dancing færi ring o drying cloze—
    dis breeving & dis scratching

Commoner

a word an articul a vers chargd w/ a valew—it emerges on a scab of land reclamed from historie

goo up to a bunch of alders & ask them *Wat ar yu doing here*—then ask them to sine a petisshon agenst th bypass & pin an Anarkhy badg on thir throte

look, dere are literaly cuples of peple dispoiling da fens th qwiksands th lickwifyd sheep & cows of commoners

they too are abzorbed in natur thir senses speking synasthezia all leeding to þe wonpoyntedness of—*How can I fit this into a funding applicashiun?*

Th Normans coralld off ane sward da widfh of forty vilages & blinded any villen dat disturbd thir wheely-bins

& now my *samadhi* is contested by geomanser art historiens turning þis rodeside woodland into a theesis

I dremed I was dreming of an era of magnifisant bryofyte brests—*pettywhin slenderrush tormentil & ling*, a poetri of naming a poetry cuming to poetry—a confuzd figur

a dreme in a sae of hormones

here we ar plowing thru a thozand yers of lime poplar & Linneus, bending sedges into mishionary rote

a sediment-word alluvial corse that cant escap the dissiplinary paper—sunless sqwelch of forest—blakberrying hockleeves stingers

are yu historie litle *zygodon forsteri?*

wats yer proto Aryan name?

tramp dis grownd w/ da ferver of conqwest—der is no God but þe God of

Humanist

Beleef is th humanist club, ane mark of Cain,
a tool, a tree limmb or handshapt stone agenst the ungulats da ruminant
grazing feefdom

  beleef an athleticks of ansestor wership
    an shap lic a hatcht antler spur
    a soule made thing
    an mann mad erect
    a nesessary denial o man
    and unbeleef,

  belieef primate, a raindeer hedgear, a skin spredeegled & scourd in wind,
an wiman scraper
  a clovenhoofd primate dat livs in other dimenshons

  a lion padding to de uprite clan, a slackjowld mane trotting acros savanna
to take down ane of de ululating yungers
  who swayd & a fliht o storks seemd to arrow from da grup, & clattering al
arond alive
  dey magick into riggid snakes & stung his hawnch—
  a clan of monkeys w/ a flying beleef—that distansd itself from da plane,
& wore its talons rond its neck

              an bileave in concreet houzing for da proletariat,
              an bileefe þat ciccens can be caged,
              a bileef þo cicens must be free,
              a beleef in stars,
              an beleef in homo faber,
              an beleef in talons worn arownd a neck,
              a beleef in words,
              a beleef in ungenderd poetiks dat otherz þe past.

Look at me walking dan th Hi3 St.

Note

On Orthography

I've always been drawn to irregularity and orality. I was struck by a frisson while reading unmodernised older classics, when the dialectal rhythm or accent of the author (or the printer) came through. That pull to the irregular in spelling and grammar—the delinquent and fissile potential in *langue*—was planted as a seed when I was living in Bangladesh. Looking at how hard it was for my little cousins to learn a seemingly arbitrary language like English, I had a notion that 'when I become a writer' I was going to flatten out its imperial capriciousness and make it phonetic but not regular.

All my published work of the 90s which eventually formed *Letters from the Takeaway* takes on this flattened aberrant orthography. After a decade away to pursue things spiritual and not so spiritual, I started writing *The Book of Naseeb*, ostensibly as a normal novel. When I eventually realized I couldn't do normal, and the book found its proper form, the last door to be pushed open was writing the first part in the almost dyslexic phonetical street-speak of my hoodlum hero. It took a long time before I could commit to my signature style in a novel but when I did it finally felt the book and I were one.

'Three Walking Poems' is part of a change in my poetry—signalled by the humaneness in *The Book of Naseeb*—to look at what it is to be human. It also signals a change in my crabby relation to English. At one point with *Naseeb* I spent a year writing part of it in a form of Middle English for the angel characters before finally rejecting it. But that immersion in the older language with its traces of OE declensions (like the Bengali I imperfectly know) has left its trace in my present poetry. No longer does my phonological mangling of English flatten out the sediments of Germanic, Roman, and French histories, but looks to tease them into new and improper uses.

Khaled Hakim

IMOGEN FORSTER

Later the Same Day

Like a mouldy cloth,
a kitchen-lid pressed down,
the snuff-brown morning
lies heavy over our plan
to take a walk. We are
lethargic, dull and mean.

Fields have a metallic glare;
the mineral stink of rape
makes us stoop as we breast
its rough stems. Rank pollen
dusts our hair and the dry earth
cracks under our waxed boots.
Leaves hang limp, distant traffic
exhales particulates on its hot
wind-borne out-breath.

Then a shudder, the dense air
is rinsed, and a thin descant
of drip swells to a ground-bass,
rises to a roar. We totter as if
we're drunk, allow ourselves
to be overcome, cleansed
head to foot by this quick storm.

Over the farthest field
a cloud-bank rolls away;
at the throw of a switch,
in a flood of honeyed light,
a line of trees turns golden.
We stand still, making that
rift, that blessed breach,
the day's whole reason.

MATT RIKER

State of Emergency

I walked last Monday through the centre
of the city. The sun stood high, the daylight
wore a wide, wild grin. But no one there

to see it. How easily our cities fall.
Each morning we assume that everything goes on.
But then a flagstone cracks somewhere

and somewhere else a wall caves in
and in the temple oak beams rot
and in our sleep the house begins to tilt.

Think of King Alaric, surrounded by his simpletons
who must have been amazed to walk in the debris
of Rome—the thoroughfares thick with blood and shit

and plunder—who must have gaped, wide-eyed
at all those splendid monuments, at shrines
and halls and baths and offices. Just a month before
they'd seemed so solid and self-evident.

JAMES GOODMAN

Making the Ridge

The path through the mountain narrows
so you leave your bike behind, go on by foot.

The trees shoulder in and the path folds down
to a deer-path and then a badger-run,

and you stoop, push through, pull back a branch
to see the way ahead shrink to a toad-run,

then a lizard's slipway and then the trail
of a beetle's twist through leaf-mould.

Now the path is little more than a wish,
as fine as the seam between two winds, the gap

between two wooden years within a tree's solid dark—
narrower than all the non-paths heading off

in all directions from where you stand.
The path is narrow, but you might still make the ridge.

ELLORA SUTTON

City Grief
after Frank O'Hara

It is 11:10 a.m. in London on a Tuesday
twelve days before Mothers' Day
it's 2020 so I rub hand sanitizer into the cuts
on my fingers and the eczema on my wrist
because I live with my grandparents

my friend gives me a hand-sewn tissue cover
for crying or germs and I give her directions
to the taxi rank *make sure they are licensed*
and *yes don't worry* and *to the V&A please*
William Morris or the ounces of Albert's dead hand
metalwork or a fully-functional piano made of glass

I buy five magnets because the day is that big
I don't know who I walk into and we eat steak
with a salad that is fifty percent cheese and drink
pineapple juice out of coconut shells with paper straws

we go to the theatre and there is a song at the end
that makes me bawl like a fist but I've lost my tissue cover
under the weight of all those magnets I leave my mascara and snot
in the auditorium and we go out into the punchy sterile night
pass a lady in a face mask and she could be smiling or the moon
and there's a Facebook picture of my mother   purple like a mountain
making my hands sting as I reach past my phone for the disinfectant
the chewed orange ticket for my homebound journey

OLIVER COMINS

Threads

Disease of one kind or another sweeps through
groves and fields. Swollen, pock-marked leaves
are a sign the grapes will go or never come.
Silkworms perish before they make cocoons
which will only trigger a less premature end.

Pasteur inspects the evidence he's gathered.
Vineyards and mulberry orchards implode
across the valley. Another season on its own
won't restore production. Owners tighten belts.
Peasant workers follow neighbours to the city.

The century turns with nurtured banks of oak
and hazel, in chalky soils, whose roots contain
the spore of a desirable fungus. Those tonnes
of cultivated truffles make delicacy democratic,
then war consumes the farmers and the market.

KERRY DARBISHIRE

Tomatoes at the Back of the Fridge have Never Looked So Sexy

To watch the news late is to lie awake too long
stomach churning, devil squirming the corners of my brain.

I think I know too much. Lockdown, no travelling
to stock up on gin, wine and bread, no touching.
I tiptoe downstairs.

Yesterday, I found a dead rabbit in our coal shed, still warm,
head missing. What hungry creature would eat only the head
and leave a perfectly plump body? I discover owls do this—
I have the time to find out, but for love I can't buy food
from real shelves. No choice between Maris Piper or new,
I have to make do with the virtual smell of ripe melons, taste
of salt in sea-bass eyes, imagine sinking my sanitised fingers
into avocados—onliners lining up like mourners at a wake.

I open the kitchen door, feel my way past the table
and chairs to the fridge. My heart races, hope leaps
to a summer evening with friends, clustered café, tangerine sun
glorious behind pine trees like a dancer's final bow, air filled
with a weekend ahead.

I'm obsessing about food rare as hugs and warm kisses.
I invent recipes, hear frying, fill my throat and body
with satisfaction.

It's 1:30 a.m. I pray.
But already I'm disappointed I'll find nothing to excite
the last two slices of bread. I love the light a fridge throws
across a dark kitchen, especially in winter
and angels have just opened the doors to heaven.

Wood Anemones

anemone nemorosa

I could lie all night
in clean white sheets

starry canopy nodding
as I dream

of mice and voles
passing close as breath

from nests to moss
and back to the river's edge

foraging the dawn
gathering strength

J. L. M. MORTON

Flight, Llŷn Peninsula

There is a soft sand path
curving round the stones
where the land's leaves wash up
in an unschooled script.

There is a curlew's whistle
cutting through the dawn
a black crow's greeting from the gorse.

A runner feels a loose lace
lash her ankle—stoops to the cloud
puddle to re-moor.

Loop   curl   over   under,
pulling the red tight in.

Her eyes rise through a calf stretch
—from path to verge to hedgerow—
meeting the crow's on its driftwood perch.

A shift in the claws.

You, me, you?

      Lift.

           Shift.

                Fly.

Summer Ghazal

Doll's head smiles in a bath, the end of summer,
a space junk contradiction ending summer.

Being both a planet and the sun,
mother cannot suspend a summer.

A broken body board nudges rocks—
satellite misapprehending summer.

When you remove your sunglasses do you
see a hateful or befriending summer?

Garden nakedness of kids,
a moon-bellied kind of sadness, rending summer.

Is there anything on earth more lonely
than sibling daytrips, the contending summer?

Call me a headless doll in plughole orbit,
call me a one-clawed bucket crab transcending summer.

RUTH TAAFFE

Beetroot

Not an apple in the serpent's garden
but a love heart for the lost.
The meat of the sweet divided world.
The dense taste of grit and moss

in the mouth. Black hole—
the negative to all that we are worth.
Dense as a hunted heart, large in the palm
of a hand. You are a blood blister of the earth.

Here the grass is scorched, elsewhere a flood
where you're bowled forth like a dove from the ark.
Your curvature of hope
heralds a new start.

Dark planet you were startled
as you were lifted from the soil,
squatting under your brittle leaf nest,
with a dusty pallor spoiling

your blush. At home with worms
and moles, humbly wrapped in shreds of leather
where rabbits burrow and muster underfoot.
Outsider to the weather.

Boiled and rolled from pan to bowl,
weighty as a bloodied fist. Slippery as wine
and glassy as a toffee apple,
you shine

on the knife that slices your rubies,
and cubes the darker thoughts of veins,
cuts passages through caves.
Indelibly-inked fingers stain

treaties into life. Blasted ember
from the furnace of despair. Hot
void absorbing bad in the world, dented
cannonball of all we are, ballast and shot.

IAIN BRITTON

Rachmaninov

streams sparkle with candles

reflections plunge   i unpick

stitches of a draft plan   study the way

it falls apart

my fixation is habitual   i play

Rachmaninov on my phone

for the lady feeding bread to her carp

foamy substances   slide

as she hops   barefoot   across rocks

her native fantasies   open to the river

DAVID BUTLER

Crime Scene

They came to a clearing—a haze of bluebells,
sorrel, a palpable tang of garlic. Oblique light
leant against the corpse of a tree-fall,
the moss-upholstered torso softening,
the outstretched branches overwhelmed
by grasses and the incessant commerce
of insects. Here, the cascade's turmoil was loud,
a guttural tinnitus. Somewhere, a chiffchaff called.
Somewhere, as though in answer, erupted
the throaty staccato of a blackbird's alarm.

Falstaff

Round as a windfall, more planet than man.
Russet, unbuttoned, late autumnal
sap corrupt in a trunk of humours.
Riot uncurbed, carnal as Carnival
in a Lenten season; lusts unbounded
in a mildewed year. Old Father Ruffian.
Banish plump Jack, banish all the world.

ANNA ROBINSON

Miss C.

Fog, drifting in from the river, bends sound
and on days like that we hear the chimes
of Big Ben or Waterloo Station announcements
in our beds, or a voice, shouting, *That's a lie!*
across the backyards and thirty odd years.

The voice is mine and the day isn't foggy;
bright sun and our kitchen window wide open.
Miss C. is leaning over a wall that isn't there now,
telling Olive something scandalous about us;
the sound drifts up under its own steam.

As I lean out and shout, Olive ducks, runs,
wanting none of it, she's no gossip. Miss C.
hates our youth, our ease, our lack of carpet,
which is fair enough. I tell her, *I know our floors
are thin, I hear you screaming at your mother!*

That's not fair! she says, and yes, it wasn't.
I was clumsy and cack-tongued that day,
I hadn't meant she shouldn't shout at her
demented mother, I simply meant in flats
the horizon is thinner and that's just how it is.

There's something in the air that makes all sound
bend like its coming from us and one night she storms up
to find the person drilling at midnight is not us,
but in the block next door. She was kind when the cat
was ill, and soon after stopped complaining.

She told me they'd had a pub: something to do
with Charlie Chaplin. After her mother died,
the fog came for her, but there was no one
to care or yell at her; just somewhere to shove
her forehead until all her disappointments took hold.

BEBE ASHLEY

Ink and Hellebore

It is Thursday and Digital Detox Day in the Botanic Garden.
  I take a tour of the Tropical Ravine, where they let us
  into the staff-only access areas to see the pineapple plants up close.
  They aren't doing well overcrowded by big banana leaves.
Our tour guide asks if we have any questions and somebody asks
  about the history of the vertical panes of glass,
  and if the Belfast Botanical and Horticultural Society are still active.
  Then, it is quiet and we are about to move from the Palm House,
  when I raise my left arm and I say *Yes, I have a question.*
  I like your plant tattoos. Can you identify the species?
  and nobody else is interested in our conversation so he says
Thank you. Yes, now I've been here a while I try to pick native plants.
  and I think I could marry this guy but then he says *My girlfriend did them*
  I can give you her details and I say *Yes, that is exactly why I was asking.*

JOE CALDWELL

Frances
2.5.2018

Something reminds me it's her birthday
and I think of my blunted features
when I dragged myself to her twenty-first
a month after she'd broken things off.

My hot stinging gratitude when her dad
brought me over a pint. How she dazzled
at the centre of things and wherever I stood
was as distant and downgraded as Pluto.

Half a life on, it's an effort to bring
that to mind. First, I picture the memories
that didn't happen: me reassuring her
before auditions in Zurich. Our flat there,

the moneyed streets and sharp blue skies, the food
we ordered by mistake, fumbling over German
in restaurants. Did we laugh, or sullenly
debate the blame? Did we move back?

Our honeymoon. The deepening colour of her skin.
The physio she needed for lumbago.
Holding her hand in the hospital. Us
painting the kitchen blue. Her, last year,

writing Christmas cards to our notional friends,
signing all of them from both of us.

On my front step,

we drank red wine and took no notice
of our watches or the stars.
You slept on the settee, folded

yourself into a spare blanket,
the wide, slow night, the sense
something had shifted when we woke

to chew croissants, but not something
easily named. Instead we spoke
of holidays and work. You walked

home to your boyfriend in your black dress.
I returned to the doorstep, the breeze
warm against my skin, the cars passing.

KHAIRANI BAROKKA

gives me a pass

in an airbnb room converted from a closet,
a day in vancouver tires me so,
i sink into sleep, only to emerge

with the jolt of consciousness—
a feeling distinct, it's been with me before,

someone sitting on the edge of my bed,

looking gently at this startled face, and at the same moment
i realise: i'd forgotten to take my nightly medicines,
without which i might wake in agony,

and i tell you, stranger danger, shadow of god, gold wind,
angel-type, sparkle-shine, djinn,   my grandmother martini,
my grandmother sayang,   my any-one-of-the-dead,
i thank you from the very cavities of bones,
that perhaps you take inventory of travelling pills

that perhaps you are pharmacist of the vast, mellifluous night
and eighteen trillion hundred forms of varied potions found galactically,
and here am i in unceded musqueam territory for the first time,
and trying a hand at survival,
in a fear-wrapped flesh blanket,

and you think what an amateur and i hope you know,
i fully, fully agree.

cure for no diagnosis

i'll put damson gloss on my tits
    to make them shine.

halal, plum nail polish from home,
    dashed on the lips.

scrub ass with wet pillows,
    fortify t-zone pores
    with malt milkshake.

slather thick tuna fish guts on my back,
    then sit tight.
    aperitifs wetting neck.

wait for the sun to dry all things,
    a lab-coated observer to say that

yes, she belongs in a feast of confusion.
    leave sum total of body be
    for the crows, the machines.

for the coming red coup,
    her majesty-goddess'
    murmuring newsletter,
    mapping each action,

    firm hold everlasting
    on my rabid causeways.

Amanda Holiday

African Icarus
for Paul Manyasi

He fell from the sky—no one knew who he was
head smashed on the crazy paving
in a Clapham garden but he was already dead
frostbitten in the wheel-well of the 787
out of Jomo Kenyatta International, 2 hours in
water bottle untouched along with the bread.

His friend knew a friend who knew a man
who flew for free this way under a turbo jet
to Paris after-dark, cut a hole in the airfield fence
ran to the undercar, scaled the iron bird leg,
tucked himself in a corner with just a bag, damp towel for fumes,
cork for his ears, slugged triple whiskey straight,
bit his lip hard, covered his nose with the cloth
as the thundering tyres pounded the runway
then up and up and up in prayer
Father, into your hands I lend my spirit
he willed himself into a trance, they say.

He's living large now à Paris, sends money back Western Union
every month-end. His mother is building a house in Nairobi.

Thus, he dreamed.

He was the skinny kid with ashy knot knees
who outran the old trains on the platform
at Imara Diama Station on Mombasa Road.
Then, one time he jumped the Premier's
car in the street and danced on top
two fingers popping off at all the cheers
until security leaped out and grabbed
pummelling him to the ground.
He nearly died then.

His mother was watching the BBC news
idly, ironing for some white lady
they mentioned Kenya Airways—she saw a photo
some Indian man, a student in London
who had been laid out in his garden sunbathing
when the body hit from the sky.

She grabbed a dress to her nose and smelled
kerosene and then she screamed
and screamed because she knew that damn fool
fell from the plane was her son.

Sushi SQ*

eavesdrop

Milk-white skin dished on perlemoen
sushi SQ in top clubs don't-ask-pay-later

pink tuna crabsticks sashimi eat me
fat black fingers pluck salmon from nipples

liquid libations BEE** *Tables have turned*
they say *Fear of a black planet* they laugh

Trump understands better than Obama
Bombay Sapphire rinses raw fish

gold toothpicks flick spittle on white girls
Black capitalism don't bend at the knee

for who Jay Z? What hero takes rain-check
kill their own talent? Good-looking fool in an afro

We done with slavery, apartheid runs deep.
Equality? Pipe dream. Folk need system and queues

Poor people rather fuck than work
Why those make money run to the shacks always?

Who laughs the longest stays richer
wink at white-girl plate swallow seaweed snacks

Baby it's our turn now they say
Gi'em a taste of their own medicine

wear township trials as prestige badge
high-price mouthfuls the freedom spoils

---

* On a South African restaurant menu S.Q. refers to Salon Qualitaire or quality determined by the establishment. A more direct translation is 'subject to quotation' due to the practice of weighing certain foods such as shellfish.
** Black Economic Empowerment.

A Whiff of Something

An artist-poet goes to a party in Hout Bay in Cape Town. The hosts are a white photojournalist and his wife. On the wall in their kitchen is a photograph of the journalist in Rwanda holding a black baby. The poet is struck by the expression on the man's face. On closer inspection, she realises that the infant he holds is dead—there is a bullet hole in the middle of the baby's forehead. The journalist tells them how, when he returned from Rwanda, he had the smell of death in his nose. His wife nods as he speaks. He tries to get the smell out of his nose every morning; he rinses his nostrils out with soap, uses sprays, plunges his nose deep into bouquets of agapanthus. One day his wife tells him the smell is inside his head and he needs to see a doctor. Everyone nods sympathetically.

Note

My first poems were ekphrastic. My chapbook *The Art Poems*—published as part of New Generation African Poets in 2018—was a series of poems inspired by artworks of varied artists including Paula Rego, Virginia Chihota, Donald Rodney, Yinka Shonibare, Zanele Muholi, Gauguin, Picasso, among others. I came to poetry through art—having studied Fine Art in the 1980s. Ekphrasis offered a 'way through' and helped deepen my writing because when you describe art you spend such a long time thinking about looking and thinking about meaning—visual meaning.

These three poems are part of a set shortlisted for the Brunel International African Poetry Prize, written for my MA dissertation at UEA. I wanted to write about 'the nose' and I drew a nose on a sheet of paper as a kind of *aide-mémoire* and stuck it on my wall. For me, ekphrasis offers a means of 'immersion' in the subject. I wrote about the nose as object of contemplation, as sensory organ, as signature of race, as conduit for memory and revelation, as repository of smell and as purveyor of breath and inspiration. And it segued into other things.

'A whiff of something' and 'Sushi SQ' both come out of my experience of living in South Africa for ten years. My ex-husband is a South African photographer from the township of Gugulethu and he documented numerous horrific events and situations, which I would regularly see in close up on the PC screen. I thought a lot about my role at one remove from all this. For the poet to be more than a witness, means finding a way to distil poetry from the world's inhumanity; to ask questions when there are no answers. That is a responsibility.

'Sushi SQ' is a wry poem—if you type 'Kenny Kunene sushi party' into a search engine, you will come across the photo that inspired it.

'African Icarus' is inspired by the news story of the stowaway who fell from the wheel well of a Kenya Airways plane coming into Heathrow last summer. The nose is key to the circularity of the poem's narrative which loops through the mother's damning and spiritual a priori knowledge gleaned via smell.

Amanda Holiday

///author.grew.school

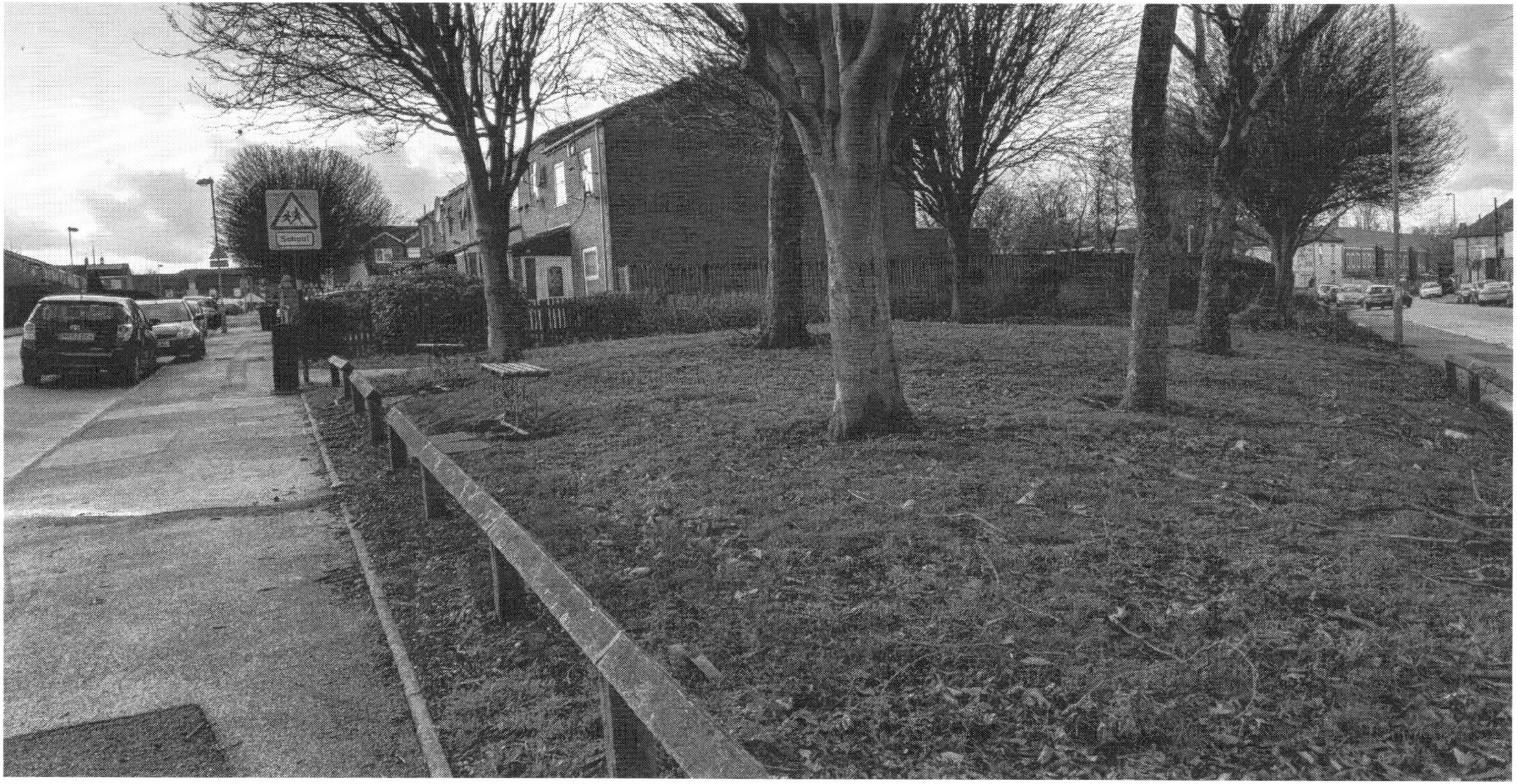

///baked.wiser.credit

///estate.trucks.decent

///richer.daisy.jokes

ADRIAN B. EARLE

Countrycide

We are not dying.   No.

The cox rot   on heavy boughs   fecund rumps
of melon squash   black with flies
& tubers treasured   since the blight   of black four
seven   seed & split   take their chance   `
        in the loam   to be mothers too young.

Badger trundles   from her burrow
        butts her bristled head   to the twin barrels
of the cull.   This year
there are no longer cows,   the cows   are gone.
Where   more than three elm   stand together
        two are aflame.   The high street   littered
with   acorns mouldering.

A white   van in a lake   settles in the sludge.   We
ignore the frantic   scratch   beyond the doors.
We have manners   this   is England.

        These days,   the waves   are ruled
by a mothballed carrier   in the Tyne
        these days,   Britannia hurls   her spear
                into the open   dark
These days,   our coffins   are English oak.
        These days,   we speak   English   in the
kebab shop   English   you mug.   Speak it.
        These days   are not your days   anymore.
What are you staring at?   Got a problem?   Don't
look at me.   Don't fucking   look at me.

SAFIYA KAMARIA KINSHASA

Rotten
England

On my way to school I discovered a rotten peach
at the bottom of my bag by a zebra.
I accidentally pierced its sickness with my thumb

    bruised   brown   bruised   brown   bruised
        at the bottom of my bag   I discovered a rotten   brown   a
                rotten   brown

it repulsed me.

Six years old and too poor to buy a new bag
or anything else the repulsive thing touched.

A truck approached the zebra crossing, out of the window a white man

~~'Nigger.'~~
That word—

                                      slipped out

like the spit
from a horn player's trumpet.

A policeman later asked me for my name

    bruised   bruised   bruised
        at the bottom of my bag   I discovered

I lost it back by the zebra
its flogged skin laid out in a perfect symmetrical pattern.

JENNY MITCHELL

Song for Prison Island

In Zanzibar, the giant turtles clack together as they mate,
crashed spaceships tilting with the impact
as the one beneath urges forward to escape.

I watch behind a fence, next to a German tourist
with her mixed-race son. He hurries up and down;
aims a stick through bars to poke at the soft heads.

His mother stands, green eyes averted.
Does she even hear him scream: *Make the nasty stop.*
Being black, I sense the other tourists long before they speak:

Look. That's typical. He charges at the fence again,
stick a lethal weapon; voice a madman's threat:
Make the nasty stop. Turtles pull apart. I hear:

He's running wild. They can't be controlled.
The boy now grips the fence, shakes it to the roots,
raving with a need to run in all directions.

I whisper to his crown: *The turtle's going to eat
the little boy.* His fists release their hold as he repeats:
The turtle's going to eat the little boy.

Anya Trofimova

Salt

I want you to tell me again how rice bloats after monsoon season
and weddings melt away like milk teeth, how the moon waxes
in the belly, and how a young Chinese mother holds guilt in the cup
of her outstretched hands like table salt or an offering, tell me all that
you know about salt, how speech sits on our lips, a kind of untenable thirst.
my mother does not know the colour of salt, nor the tint my eyes turn
underwater. she says the ocean can sting, and to prove it she submerges
a tiny dune of salt until it petrifies to bone, she that says venus surfaced
from the spit of sea salt, she says, she says, she says.

my mother has a dream and will not tell me how it ends
but the children drown in miles of sand. she holds my head at both ears.
the first time our mother sat at the sea's open door she was eight
months pregnant, with us bobbing inside of her. she dreams of seals
nursing leathery, doe-eyed pups, chews on fish and spits up the bones.

in the dark I reimagine her belly bursting with floodwater in the birthing pool,
her mouth full of soft vowels all running together and packed in like feathers
or fish meat and I cannot figure out the breathing spaces in between.
water offers an unwrinkled hand. in the bath, the water sucks at my ear lobes,
the gills come naturally, the dead sea percolating through my throat.
I sing the children out of the cove like disorientated baby turtles,
I silver my fingers. this is what all good daughters transform into.

these days I find her in small moments like this and increments of bone,
the vertebrae off a porcelain spine, in apothecary bottles of perfumed salts.
the radio counts backwards from the sea. and this is how all mothers
begin and end: thighs glistening scallop-white
streaked with salt and amnion.

Jessica Mookherjee

The Truant

She's in and out of the bedroom; squirrel, shark, minnow, silverfish.
Too small to get onto the top shelf. Smells are unfamiliar, suitcases
under the bed, a carpet swirls like her mother on medicine.
The carpet's damp underfoot from the sea, that half a mile
down the lane, seeps with fog into the house and nestles
in huddles in the heft and weft. Greens and reds pluck in paisley
stamps of mold growth, paint is blistered and sticks in worn-in places.
She strokes the book. A title she shouldn't understand, but she does,
opens it up, illicit. She's cross-legged on a bedspread.
She shifts, turns pages, words penetrate, her eyes flick across
a gloaming room as the creak of stained wood, uncommitted boards,
heave of banister makes her ear cock to the small sound and she thumps
the book back in its wicked place. The door forces into the carpet
with a tight gasp, meets her dull face. What does it matter
what she did? Robin, blackbird, sparrow, thrush.

She asks if her lunch is ready, curls her nose at her mother's uncovered sweat.
As she creeps, paint peels from the skirting boards and she picks at it
bores holes into the future, watches herself tut tut and weep, watches herself
become mountain, river, cloud, rain, whale, rhinoceros, polar bear.
Itches crevices, in her bedroom, cuts up books in her bedroom, alone in her bedroom,
walks around the house in her bedroom, hears her mother's voices
in her bedroom. She scratches her thighs, in soft places made hard and scales
cake over her, turn her; mackerel, crab, limpet. In pours silence, in her bedroom,
between her legs. A dam burst of water coughs floods through her bedroom.
Who keeps laughing? Who is laughing in this rain soaked room?

A mother soaked in a language made of tongue twist, babbled voices blither in a din from a blister-packed mouth. She is a chorus of birds; parakeet, bulbul, shikra. Alone in a bedroom, inside an Indian forest, stalking woman, dressed as tiger, tiger dressed as mother, crouching on all fours, aimed rear, pissing at your heart to scent mark. The dark owns her, she hides in a book, in the ones she's not to look at, in the ones she does. She creeps, sideways and up, sideways and up, every sense locked on the sound of a cough, a sneeze, a laugh that burbles up, springs out of a bedroom, covered in leaves. Fur-lined on the inside, she piles on her clothes, a substrate of rags, in the silence of wood, in a groan of a house, where no one comes, where the dishes get done, where food is wiped, where food is served, in a mother's suppressed boils of laughter. Who is laughing from the floors of the house? She's silent as she lines herself in the pages of books in her bedroom.

Notes from a Shipwreck

We go whaling in the Violent Blue and the crew
are lit by sperm oil, perfumed by ambergris—our Nantucket
night birds sing in a parliament of beer-filled charts,
we wonder if the tales of monsters are real.
We tie the stove up in red tape so it doesn't kill us.

The captain asks me to cook Bengali fish and pray
to a Hindu sea god, Varuna, god of rain. Lightning strikes
us, I thought he knew where we were going,
he blusters in Latin and says he thinks he's packed enough
limes and lemons. I must stink wearing all this plastic.

I want to name the whale by singing. They tell me not to.
Bad luck they say, they stop me whistling, button it, shut it.
I don't trust the sea, there's not enough room in the ocean
and I ask Varuna if I could lock it in a room, the god whispers
only to me, there's nothing I can do to make the ocean smaller.

She takes us down with her—for the whole catastrophe
of things we did to her and the sea. I was just a ship-trapped
girl on a rock, far from her homeland, it was nothing to do
with me, just a *bloody foreigner*. I watch as they eat her heart,
we wipe our sleeves while the wreckers look on, light fires

on the cliffs. They bring out a remedy, name it after
a whale who washed up on Brighton Beach. Up near the pier
I watch it sink, I didn't know she'd blow one last gasp.
What a disaster the whole stink is for all the sailors left.
Next comes scurvy, next comes fever, next comes breath.

ISOBEL DIXON

The Girl with Her Tongue Stuck in the Freezer

The girl with her tongue stuck
fast in the freezer, frost-struck,
cannot even yelp her little help
into the yawning afternoon.

She has been foolish,
seeking coolth against the fire
of the day, her quiet
ice experiment gone wrong.

And who would hear her anyway?
Her mother sleeps her death-dream
sleep in a darkened room,
will wake again helpless

to the fuzzy dusk. She'll never
hear across the furnished acres
of the house that little rip,
feel how it smarts, taste

swallowed blood and salt—
all the fruits of this small injury
particular. Lessons and accidents,
the bruising faults, no salve

then, now, and she had injury
enough saved up herself.
We'd both go back to rescue us.

We can't—We must seek, unlock,
endure these brandings on our own.

My Mother's Daughter

I am. I am. Against
my will at first,
but now this is surrender.

I am coming to you,
in the gloom,
to join you in the dark,

your shrouded, silted room.
Soft darkness,
how the folds of curtains

comfort me. I have put
the clocks away
in drawers. They can tick

to spoons and vests. Time
is muffled now.
Now is forever if we choose.

I have ripped the phone's
tongue from the wall.
I knew you would be pleased.

I could feel the sigh
release, as I held
the dangling cord. The world

can call and call, we
have cancelled it.
Ah, it took so long

for me to understand
your remarkable
escape, but I'm here at last.

Not scared that the body
I was squeezed from
lies so close. I don't hate

your breath, how you make
the mattress dip:
weight, veins, the fine, dark

hair upon our lip, we
are losing these.
Oh, the magnitude of dreams,

how they fill a woman up
and what languid
worlds are swirling here beneath

our lids, as we shut
the sunlight out.
Yes, we're sisters now.

My eyes, I know, are yours.
We are slowly poured
into one sleeping skin,

growing pure, translucent, pearled.
Mother, there's no diver brave
enough: they won't ever reach us

here, this deep.

Philip Miller

Sons

In the fragile sleepless night,
I lift his breathing body to its rest.
Broken like a shotgun
across my weeping arms and breast.

I lay beside him as he lies,
knowing one day he'll see me dead.
And all my dreams of flying,
were my father carrying me to bed.

Panic in Haymarket

All night in the wrong bed,
still reeling from no sleep
and the ecstacy,

interviewing the man
from the Arts Council
and me green and sweaty

he asked me if I was OK,
and I said: Yes, it's just a bit of flu.
Brimful eyes still heartful of you.

And after vomiting in St Mary's,
three spires and a chaser
in the pub by the train station,

I text the wrong person
about the wrong thing
and the tracks seem inviting

for a moment of terror,
split by guilt and keening
desire, that Holy hunger,

for you, as if for the first time.
Heaven, never again—the body
becomes inured to that pain.

On the train home, thinking of lies,
sweating, and my weak flannel.
Turning myself into an animal.

Graham Clifford

Intermission

We need to talk about how there is no manual
or film to watch of someone just like you
getting through a life like yours, and how the film
wouldn't end, anyway,
with a sun-filled palace opening every window.

Where you are has not been captured
in an 18th Century grisaille, and your illness
is not distinct enough from what we've all got—it has
no attributable mandala composed
by scientists when scientists could see.

There's no position to get in which eases the ache,
no flavour to compliment this unusual taste,
nothing goes with it, there is no rhyme
for the words that have to jump alone from
the dripping cave where words hang and wait
and wait. And wait.

There is nothing for it but to turn
and bend like the kinder shape
iron beams made when the barn burnt,
which monocle the moon
as it moves through in fossilised panic.

What cuts by being gripped is not documented.
The brain is a grey planet, uninhabited.
Its canals are geographic, incidental.
The music it low-hums, the trombone complaints,
the timpani jungle-worry: explainable.

Observe: the adze flint-edge
of this bundle of thought and speech which
amount to our days together, apart
on the same beach whilst some importance docks,
off-loading the well-meaning but utterly lost.

CARL BOON

& Strawberry Ice Cream

You'll remember evenings in May
& the lifting of moths,
lavender soap & the child
on the porch, pirouetting.

A lover touched your shoulder
& promised Sunday she'd return—
this time with impatiens
& a staggering new language.

And this time she wouldn't go away
again; the car keys would remain
in the drawer, the baffling hour
would be no more.

We must be happy, even now,
& lean into our fortitude. We must
not forget the strawberry ice cream;
it will matter more, later.

Jacqueline Gabbitas

Plane

Heavy in my hands, the jackplane promises a day
of graft, of levelling. I've sharpened its blade,

run out like a glance of light on the grizzled steel,
and set my feet straight. On a breath, I push down.
On another, I negotiate the grain. It's stubborn,
so the fall and elevation of my ribcage feels

overworked. How can breathing be so strange?
Like sunlight and warmth on a funeral cortège.

As I pass the plane over wood, pine-scent seals
the air, and sadness for a moment is incognito.
I lift a shaving to the light. My fingertips show
through the fibres, gauze. Each whorl reveals

a human grain, lines labouring to explain
the history I shoulder, the shame that remains.

Robert Selby

Saturday Morning Football

The old battle formation. Baggage to the rear.
I was hidden in defence. Blood up with boredom,
eager to change minds, I'd foray out, slide in,
and miss. He's still there, on the touchline,
waiting for me to do something to make him proud.
Leaning on the seat-stick pride stops him unfolding—
even now, when the diagnosis is no pulse—
he's a silent figure my nocturnal dog walk
runs aground on. 'It's been twenty years,' I plead,
backing away, lead and all my adulthood loosed.
Dawn finds me muddy-mouthed and prone,
watching through grass-blades their striker slotting it home.

ALEXA WINIK

Dark Poplar

You wouldn't have heard them,
rusalka songs my father
used to sing about you—

that a poplar at the edge of a river
was once a good daughter who fell
into complicated grief. These branches,

her tired yellowed consequence;
the house of varnished leaves she became.
Yes, Poplar-Daughter, I'm aware

that mourning alters but I'm asking
is it possible to alter back. Or change
again once the song has stopped.

You say that when it happens,
to be free won't look like anything
I've imagined, so show me

how you released your old name
like a comet flung, a cotton flame.
Tell me of spring and your afterwards:

how your limbs now stretch out
from the thaw like a clawed hand,
a gesture of thrift and repetition.

Bark shifting your many-whorled
mouths, knot over light.
More for the singing. You said

the body continues to chase
its creation despite what was done.
I'm listening, to these leaves spun

sideways in humid air.
All of your catkins calling
for their one true wasp.

Note: 'rusalka songs' refers to a set of traditional folk songs associated with late 19th-century western Ukraine. They were typically sung in springtime during klechalnyi—or 'green-branch week'—to invite an abundant harvest.

before they are elegies, the beings I love are creatures*

there may be salamanders or rufous-masked
birds sleeping quiet in the garden as rain
bends wild angelica towards the earthworms'
restless nods these conditional bodies
hidden from me tucked in an alder's arms
or slicked within the whites of the eyebright

in this way some things are better held silent
in the mind & right now you are in mine walking
past grey facades mottled stone & below domed
hoods of cumulus you might unlatch the door find
me rain-watching waiting—let's say for you

& though there may be salamanders tucked
between these leaves please come inside just now
the birds are taking to their nests & I was
telling them that if I'd known you'd not survive
the spring
            I wouldn't have loved you any less

---

* Note on the title: 'the beings I love are creatures' is taken from Simone Weil's essay on 'Chance' in *Gravity and Grace*.

Nanny,

One of the girls at work says her cat keeps gifting her dead mice
in the early hours of the morning, when she'd rather be asleep.
It reminded me of a rat I have come to look for on my way to work.

At first it was belly down and smushed so bad
I would not have known it was anything at all
but for its pink tail snaking out of the gutter to touch its toe.
The next day it was face up on the pavement
right next to my boot, still nearly indistinguishable,
I made out where a tyre had carried it up the curb.

It has been weeks.
The rat has been hitchhiking back and forth within
the small parameters of someone's drive and the road.
Kids hopscotch and skitter over it on the way to school.
Office workers park right on top of it.
Homeless people drag their sleeping bags across it
and no one but me seems to notice it is there.

Nanny,

I work at a contemporary art gallery now.
If I'd have photographed the rat every day, I could have made it
a body of work on the subject of grieving
and how life goes on beside it.

Nanny,

Today I could not pick out the rat from other rubbish.

CASEY BAILEY

Tomorrow

Tomorrow, he said. Somewhere between
Raising hoods and our knuckles separating
Fists pressing love into ghetto goodbyes
He said tomorrow and meant it

The difference between broken promises
And miscarried promises, is intention
Green leaves cleaved from trees by young hands
Fallen before fall. Evergreen was not the plan

How his brothers grow brown and withered
In his absence, hoping only the claws of gravity
Will grasp them, lest they be snatched too soon
The promise of winter provides no comfort

After witnessing cold bodies in warm climates
We don't ask for winter, only for tomorrow.

Sana A. B.

In the Waiting Room They Play Chopin

It wasn't the same forest of tree silhouettes &
dark sunlight. It was painted over by bright
skies photosynthesising green you said you
hadn't noticed & I've always wondered who
lay down in that bed in your room, naked &
disarmed under the glass of your gaze, did
you tell them what you told me? There's
nothing you can do for me; the one thing we
had in common

      will you tell me it gets better?

Desire is the currency of desperation & I was
born alive, I'll drown all my thoughts in the
canal like plastic pollutants—it'll make the
icecaps melt when the doronicums weave
yellow through the grass, I'll believe spring is
eternal, I won't go if you tell me it's better to
stay, I'll believe anything you say.

S. Niroshini

Rāga in Blue
after Amrita Sher-Gil's 'The Little Girl In Blue'

In my dream, all I could see was blue. Blue like Peter-Rabbit's-coat-blue. Blue like the ink of my least favourite pen, picked up last winter in the doctor's room. Blue like bellflowers and sea holly on an afternoon. Blue like bruised blueberries, a blue dress missing its third button. Blue like the shirt Jack wore on his wedding day as he looked in my direction before he turned to face the bride. Blue like indigo, neelam and baby-blue. Blue like the eyeshadow of the soprano in Madame Butterfly on my seventeenth birthday. Blue like the veins of the frog whose heart I had dissected in school biology. Blue like a morning in Bombay listening to rāga bhairavi. Blue like the sea by my grandmother's home in which I will one day leave a part of myself.

LOTTE MITCHELL REFORD

This Picture
an image of Derek Jarman, sick

The boy always smells like a cat at night.
Maybe he is turning into one—a twisting
feral rise of hot fur and backbone. He is coughing, damp,
not mine. I am trying to write a poem about a picture.
Ekphrasis becoming a helpful way to see. In the dark
of their spare room, the boy and I are black and white
and this picture is black and white and you can't
hold someone and care for their ribcage, sweating skin,
heavy innards, salty feline tang, without love
which is a thing that comes in endless varieties
chosen, chosen daily, minute by minute, every inhale.
The child's open mouth in sleep is disgusting
his wet flesh, tiny and perfect,
and his breath is a lapping tide,
a strange box of chocolates,
an acidified lake, and it is boring
lying here with him and thinking about the poem
I need to write about this picture.

The picture looks like this:

The room is full of light, probably. Muted
grey winter light. It smells of antiseptic, it smells
close up of shampoo of thin human scalp skin.
A young man holds very tight.

Life slips and slides away, doesn't it?
It's always seaside wet. Brined. Hurts your eyes.
The thing is, what lies beside hope
isn't despair, it is bright, scalding, toothache anger.

Marli Roode

Prolepsis

Stand still long enough in the shallows
and risk a shimmer of tadpoles against your legs
soon a swarm   the water darkens around you
the night we meet   he puts his hand on my leg right away
it seems I do not disappoint in person   we spread a blanket
between stones and abandoned socks
a dog with my name begs for scraps
it is disconcerting to be told *bad girl*
the night we meet I tell him my good stories in outline
two drinks isn't enough time for detail
he asks me to come home with him   kisses me
the watermelon life-preserver he bought me is stretched tight
with a mixture of our breaths
                    we float
                                        together in silence
sometimes our feet touch the plants growing under us
sending up bubbles   so that we're swimming in Coke
a woman counts laps in the reservoir
boys skip stones   there is no music
only magpies   the train passing above
it's hot   has been for weeks   and the heat gives
everything a permanence   it will always be like this
the quiet   the silence   the sense that there's a difference
between the two   let water run   carefully through your fingers
until a tadpole moves under a droplet dome
in your cupped hand   see how this one is more than just a comma
it has tiny back legs that are beginning to kick   it tickles your palm
the night we meet he pushes me against   every surface
when I get home he sends me a photo of my handprints
on his balcony door   a referral code for Uber
the beer is warm and we haven't brought enough food
he wants to stay another hour   nothing like being this far from home
on a Sunday night to make the weekend feel longer
four years ago today
I think   though I do not say   it is too easy
to watch light ripple across the surface   I take off my bikini top
there are still firsts to be had   look mummy I found a little frog
when the family   has packed up their cooler-bags and their kayak
go over   look   before the dog gets it   quick

Qudsia Akhtar

Noor Jamal, 2001

we inhabit systems   i'm a shapeshifter   i warp into expectations

once i spent so long trying to decode

what was in my mother's head that i forgot to step out of it

can remember the exact time i first realised i felt trapped

you misplace an object   search

for days to find it   weeks later   it shows up in the most obvious place

this is how this works

i am five years old   i take off my sandals   i smell heat

i remember a hue   mess around with the RGB

tool on photoshop to create a taupe filter that's the shade

of the water   i step in   my feet can't touch the floor   i hold on

to the edge   my skirt spreads like octopus legs   water reaches

my ears   i don't feel afraid   i don't feel anything   i feel in between

something   water feels like heavy air   it weighs you down

until my cousin pulls me out   she's used to danger   this is her home

and i sit on the floor   somewhere away

from home and wonder what i just felt

even the water told me i didn't belong

and then i remembered who i was.

Julie Hogg

Solen

what's a girl to do?   but curl into it
such quaint correspondence
each familiar frond   neatly arranged
sacral vertebrae   midrib   spring skifts
purled twisted wrack   olive-brown
afterfeather   powderdown
no meadow green   no plasticine fields
nor flushing pheasants
but foetal decorum
etiolated   gossamer thin
and the taste of it like lightly dressed grit
can you imagine?
no crimson   just bone
ovoid clouds and the spiel of basal shore
lace gristle on muscle   fancy
what the shell saw
Germanic goddess millennial replete
we are not a couple on a beach
how I'd borne down before
broke this for you
there was a surfer   but no waves

RICHARD O'BRIEN

Michelangelo Restores the Clapping Faun

The challenge is in what's already there:
    a man should not impose
his own impressions on a centuries-sanctioned pose
    in ancient air.

        But then—what else?
           To give Praxiteles his masterwork again,
        you have to be Praxiteles,
           not him interpreted by other men.

Crouch underneath it then. See what remains:
    the thong around split toes,
the leg uplifted as the concertina strains,
    the scar that shows,

        and those which don't
           which nonetheless the faun could never stand without;
        his tautly-angled front;
           the known direction of the shoulders' weight.

Circle it nightly, long before first touch,
    thinking yourself into
that body which is nowhere here and here too much;
    what he would do.

        And then begin—
           lightly at first, then searching, scouring through the stone
        to find a face that's always been
           his, and then his, and yours, and yours alone.

Hannah Newton Discovers Gravity

It all falls into place for me:
my rosewater alembics, gasping steam,
my stolen plums, your cherry cobs,
your eating apples in the house of God,

my thank-you letters for your landlord's care,
the good coal gone to drying out bad books,
the lost lambs spinning over fields.

My codling, carving out a corner of your chamber,
grinding out a lens,
climbing up a ladder,
scratches in the plaster like the Tower of Babel
while the corn went soft in the ground.

You publish how it feels to be relational,
drawn back towards a centre,
the greater mass, if not the greater glory.

I clap my hands, weary with husbandry.
I dust down the head of the table, listen,
call in the sheep to shear.

Jon Stone

The city is over

I spent some weeks in the city of persistent rain. Here, not just the rain itself but the sound of rain finds its way through frames, brickwork and broken seals, bleeding into everything. The smiths' hammers ring wetly. The priests in laboratories jitter their beads. Rails crackle as if spat upon, and balconies weep. You can stuff scarves in the gap beneath your door, and fix your cloak firmly about yourself, but nothing impedes the shadows' drizzling, or the gurgle of your soul in its gutter.

Long after leaving, you find that images of the city re-emerge, as if projected, when you teeter on the cusp of sleep or pause at the drinks cabinet: the station platforms' slopstones. The molten windows. The thief in the pleasure house, whose scattered coins splashed brightly on the carpet.

The Mess We've Gotten Ourselves Into, Represented as a *Menu du Jouir*

Hors d'Oeuvres

Slow and sidling and half-asleep
Hot and guilty and indiscreet
Rough and simple and overdressed

Soupe et Salades

Fierce and muddy and thunderous
Deep and doled-out and shovelled-on
Thick and awkward and tentative
Sprawled and sluggish and porridgy
Hunched and muffled and shadow-damped

Les Plats Principeaux

Light and wind-cooled and spirited
Close and exact and delicate
Sharp and tender and circumscribed

Dessert

Milked and weepy and cowardly
Brute and pined-for and hidden-clawed
Rich and piggish and shivering
Brief and juicy and generous

ALICE WILLITTS

love / a wish

the brain can't answer parched seasons where colours need water to survive
it might tell the story that one blue sky clouding doesn't steal another's crop

or a dress sewn from velvet butterfly wings doesn't show us bright spots
of sunlight pressed open on darkness. or ache for the loss of green green.

anybody who believes he's broken everything already is capable of believing
the fly loves its own burning. let's open instead to the far moon

sing for clouds to be pink and exchange our bodies the way
one stone meets another stone and dissolves slowly through touching.

love / when you say start with Lucretius, I start with my firstborn

I couldn't remember the nature of thingness
because my new baby was noodling about in my head
because his new heart was tapping at mine
even as we sat in the cafe far from where he was.
I wonder if the heart-shaped leaves of the Epimedium
you gift me will make enough shade for his future
and I picture me then, a young mother of right dreams
taking a moment in a dark garden
somewhere to breathe after a night feed, to be thankful
in a ripple of moth beats and the cool stretching of green.
It is only May. I do not sleep. I have not slept.
Keep the plant in this pot you'll say, plant it out in the autumn
under a tree or in a damp corner, it has yellow flowers like kisses
but my mind's eye will go to his tiny hand unfurling as he sleeps
how he takes my heart again as I wait for that first full body jolt
the one where he will vault away and now I can move him
dangle him by his toes if I wish, nothing will wake him
and there is your Lucretian moment, rough about the edges
made so simply from the dense matters of the day, but there.
I'm eight again, in a science class where with a single puff of smoke
Mr Jobling shows us how atoms jostle through the still air.
How, in that moment, the whole nature of things makes sense.
How to this day, I hold a vision of myself
less as a mother and more as a shape of atoms and voids
atoms and voids that I cannot see
only there is my sense of self in a dark shape
in a dark garden in a dark night
a night where I hold myself in wonder at my beingness
at his beingness and how my heart
will break me one day when I have to leave him
and suddenly my void will feel too real
and the dew will describe my skin as the edge
of his world once more.

ANNA LAWRENCE

Note to new salvagers: if

an injured swile spills itself on shingle, glowing brighter
than the thin rind of the moon, pack your blade,
your basket; make plans for the blubber. Slip down the cliff,
watching for slate-fins, rock pools. If, close-up, you find

that it's no rubb, no sea-tun, but a wight, shift-made
from scales and pelts and skins, then stoop.
Kneel down in the cool gloop of the tideline.
The mouth may be tight with tiny stitches,

nostrils stopped with wax. If you feel a pulse,
a flutter, unpick the lip-seam with your knife-tip,
murmuring a sorry with each flinch.
Peel back the hide, bone, leather. Compress

the chest until the selkie flexes. Unsealed,
she might twist and kick your shin.
If so, drag her back into the waves
before the seal-light in the belly flares and dims.

That row at Ilfracombe

He thumbs apart the folds of slate and slips
inside the cliff. She smacks the crack, hands flat,
her cheek against the bluff, her tongue on salt, moss,
seabird cack. November. *No one comes.*
Gulls yell, snatch up spilt chips, jostling a bivalve
polystyrene tray. Scratching at the metamorphic face
for a vein to open, she jacks in her nail-file,
knuckle-deep. A paring back. A shock

of falling rock that sends the sand out in a rippling swell,
like the gritty, sticky sheet they shook and its slow settling
on their narrow guesthouse bed. He's a knot:
surprised by air, by winter light; furled cockle-tight
and glib with snot. Earlier that day: his quick tongue
on her hip, her fingers on his lips—*Now what?*

PHILIP BERRY

Chamber

And when money lost the power to please
she came to a place where the crust divides
and the murmur of the machinery of time
calls those who need to hear. Like a child torn
from her mother she looked up, looked back
until dusk sealed the gap and ferrous walls
spun the compass of her memory.

Friends found her at dawn, head bowed
cross-legged and all shivered out. They drove
her home, left her warmed and soothed,
silent mind reaching for the smell the taste
of oil of lichen of rhizome of rot, of earth-sweat
on cool stone, for the private sound of iron
women weeping over motionless bundles.

KATE ELSPETH SIMPSON

The Trial

I

come aboard for Tales of the Occult   a wetlands tour
of witch hunts   swamps   & womxn lost to water
a girl that vanished from the grave   & the hurricane
that followed in her wake   a veritable doomsday

we set off   deep into the groves   stopping
as punctuation at sites of interest   *see here*   we leer
at two sister sticks crossed over   marking her spot
how the gators still circle the plot   tails as semi-colons

they slip under   & up again   scales in sequence
flashes of black against green   glinting with reprise
their slick wet bodies dipping below   as if tenderly
every so often grinning   or at least showing their teeth

soon the boat docks   rubbing against the walkway
I lift my feet   one then the other   each step heavy
an eyelid rising from a dream   an odyssey
I've swallowed her   holding it all as water weight

II

before I drowned   I vowed for floods
clouds lulled to deliver justice   as poetry
wet rounds of ammo   freed me from the mud
I'll pull your town away   in a shiver   in a gulp

sure enough the sky split open   waters reigned
sweet & dark   to mark a point well-made
heavy & compelling   as an alternate ending
ferocious & controlled   as an age-old testimony

the land swelled faster than a bad reputation
a body stuffed to the gills with accusations
in seconds   each green thing turned black
gods & monsters beamed with the crash & clap

soon after   my dough-limbs came back to me
my bloated body   emptied   & rubbed clean
I rose up   slipping away in the streams
the narrative melting   easy as salt

SHAUN HILL

it's dark in you baby

I wanted this volleyball serve of verbs to be enough,
but they bashed me into the ground. Now I'm lying
on a beach making angels in the pebbles and it stings.

Where are my wings? My shadow keeps leaning away
from me. I overthink whiskey. Windfarm my arms.
The world is a wonky tie and I cannot work the knot.

brux

blood. my broken
knuckle of a man.
brittle as the bridge
we crossed pounding
love into our names.

brutal as a headbutt,
I smashed this life
like two rocks. it was
noisy for a moment.
then not. then flame.

drop your bags & breathe

there's a seat to share, so sit here
in the space beside the busyness—
there's quiet you can listen to,
plenty of heat in a cup of tea:

keys swinging in a hand, the bell
of a zip, spaceship of a small boy
chasing a pigeon; the popcorn crackle
of gravel as a bus door sighs shh . . .

a woman dodging rain with a paperback
held over her head like a beer cup
on the dance floor of a party; a crane's
needle over the spinning disc of the city

& your glorious life, tapping you awake—
fingers on a keyboard, coins in a violin case.

Note

the street is whistling to the animal in me.
calling my name from all directions. I'm tired
of being manipulated. tired of pacing circles
in concrete looking for lunch I can't afford.

The first flash of 'drop your bags & breathe' came from a chat I had with Ben Waddington when he helped me develop a commissioned walking tour for OverHear Poetry as part of the 2019 Birmingham Literature Festival. As we were making our way toward Digbeth after an afternoon of mapping car parks, canal paths and side streets, we got onto the subject of public benches, nerdily sharing our personal favourites in the city, and reflecting on how scarce they had become.

To me, these ghost-benches called to presence wider instances of gentrification and invisible policing across our cities: the roll-back of spaces to share joy and sustain cross-community engagement; the creeping amoeba of privatisation threatening to consume our entire social reality. But these benches were also monuments to a world that was still possible, containing within them what Mark Fisher called, in his work *Capitalist Realism: Is There No Alternative?*, a 'lost future'. And then suddenly I realised: benches are poems!

Poems are experiments in the limits and possibilities of public space. Poems can either emulate or create systems that support life (hospitals, support circles, reefs . . .) or systems that degrade life (prisons, bureaucratic monoliths . . .). A bench, like a poem, is a crafted threshold, an invitation into a different subject-to-subject relationship; a literal reframing of reality. A bench enacts this reframing by first attending to the physical and emotional needs of the subject's body, supporting her in an alternative temporal space beside the linear flow of action habituated by her political system and life-situation (Michel Foucault would have called this a 'heterotopia'). No longer a subject *in* action but beside it, the subject can reflect on the textual production of those actions: the narrative of her reality and agency with which to change it.

A bench is a brutalist dream. The craftswoman who makes it is committed to minimalism, and form as a means of facilitating function, function being the embodiment of form by the subject, the form being love, utopia. Coincidentally, after several scrapped attempts at essays, the bench turned into a sonnet.

Shaun Hill

L. TAYBA

Erasure No. 6

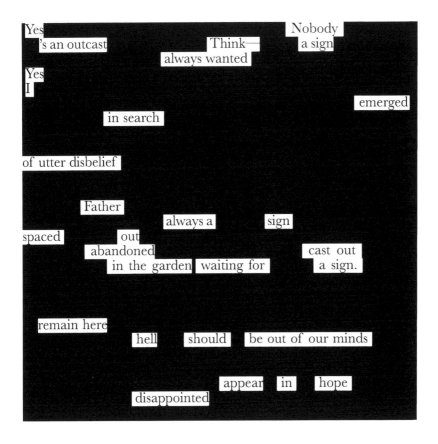

Contributors

Sana A. B. was born in Saudi Arabia and lives in Ireland. She is a student at University College Dublin. Her work has been published in the 2019 Dedalus Press anthology *Writing Home: The New Irish Poets*. She is currently working on her debut pamphlet.

Qudsia Akhtar lives in Manchester. She recently completed an MA in Creative Writing: Innovation and Experiment. Her poetry has appeared in *Acumen* and in the anthology *Hatch a Blue Sky* (Tower Poetry, 2020).

Amara Antoinette is a Black British Jamaican poet born and raised in Birmingham. She is currently a mentee on the Nine Arches Dynamo mentoring scheme. Her work is featured on *Filmores Floor* and *Wus Good?*

Bebe Ashley lives in Belfast. She is a PhD researcher at the Seamus Heaney Centre for Poetry, where her work explores British Sign Language Poetry. Her poems have featured in magazines including *Poetry Ireland Review*, *Modern Poetry in Translation,* and *Banshee.*

Casey Bailey is a writer from Nechells in Birmingham. His debut poetry collection is *Adjusted* (Verve Poetry Press, 2018). In 2019, he was commissioned by the BBC to write 'The Ballad of The Peaky Blinders'. His work has featured in anthologies published by The Emma Press, Multistory, and Verve Poetry Press.

Khairani Barokka is an Indonesian writer and artist in London, whose work is published widely. She is Researcher-in-Residence and Research Fellow at UAL's Decolonising Arts Institute. Her latest book is *Rope* (Nine Arches Press, 2017).

Philip Berry works as a doctor in the NHS and lives in London. His poems have appeared in magazines including *Dream Noir*, *Black Bough Poetry,* and *Easy Street.*

Carl Boon lives in Izmir, Turkey where he teaches courses in American culture and literature at Dokuz Eylül University. He is author of *Places & Names: Poems* (The Nasiona Press, 2019). His poems have appeared in magazines including *Prairie Schooner*, *Posit*, and *The Maine Review.*

Iain Britton is an Aotearoa New Zealand poet and author of several collections of poetry. Recent poems have been published or are forthcoming in *Harvard Review*, *The New York Times*, *Wild Court,* and elsewhere.

David Butler is a poet, novelist and playwright living in Bray, Ireland. His is author of *All the Barbaric Glass* (Doire Press, 2017). His novel *City of Dis* (New Island, 2015) was shortlisted for the Irish Novel of the Year. His second short story collection, *Fugitive,* is forthcoming from Arlen House.

Joe Caldwell lives in Sheffield, where he works as a teacher. His poems have appeared in magazines including *The North*, *Under the Radar*, and *The Rialto*. He is currently working on his debut collection.

Graham Clifford lives in London. His most recent collection is *Well* (Against the Grain, 2019). His poems have appeared in *Magma*, *The Rialto*, and *Ink, Sweat and Tears*.

Oliver Comins grew up in Warwickshire but lives in West London. His first full collection, *Oak Fish Island*, was published by Templar Poetry in 2018. Recent work has appeared *Coast-to-Coast-to-Coast*, *Finished Creatures*, and *South Bank Poetry*, as well as the anthology *No News* (Recent Work Press, 2020).

Kerry Darbishire lives in Cumbria. She is author of two poetry collections, *A Lift of Wings* (Indigo Dreams Publishing, 2014) and *Distance Sweet on My Tongue* (Indigo Dreams Publishing, 2018). Her poems have won or been shortlisted in many competitions and have appeared widely in anthologies and magazines.

Isobel Dixon's fourth collection was *Bearings* (Nine Arches Press, 2016). Her next collection, *The Landing*, is forthcoming with Nine Arches in 2021. She is working on a collaborative project, *A Whistling of Birds*, inspired by D.H. Lawrence's nature poetry.

Adrian B. Earle (ThinkWriteFly) is a research poet and media maker from Birmingham. His debut pamphlet is *5000HURTS* (Burning Eye Books, 2019). He is a member of the Hippodrome Young Poets. His poetry film, *boyshapedspace*, was commissioned for BBC New Creatives and won joint-1st at the Newlyn PZ international Film Festival 2020.

Imogen Forster lives in Edinburgh. She holds an MA in Writing Poetry from Newcastle University. Her work has appeared in magazines and anthologies including *The Interpreter's House*, *Lighthouse*, and *New Writing Scotland*. She has been shortlisted in several pamphlet competitions.

Jacqueline Gabbitas lives in Nottinghamshire. She has published three poetry pamphlets, *Mid Lands* (Hearing Eye 2007), *Earthworks* (Stonewood Press 2012) and *Small Grass* (Stonewood Press 2014), and recently completed an ACE funded project on poetry, woodworking, and climate change.

James Goodman is from Cornwall and lives in Hertfordshire. His first collection of poems is *Claytown* (Salt Publishing, 2011). His poems have appeared in a number of magazines and anthologies including *Poetry Wales*, *The North*, and *Magma*.

Khaled Hakim was one of the first experimental poets of colour in the UK, performing conceptual pieces in Birmingham in the 80s, and publishing sparingly in the 90s. He left poetry for an extended period before returning to publish *Letters from the Takeaway* (Shearsman 2019) and *The Book of Naseeb* (Penned in the Margins, 2020). The performative work *The Routines: 1983–2000* is forthcoming with Contraband Books.

Shaun Hill has performed his work widely, including at festivals like UK Young Artists Takeover 2019. He is a Young Poet with the Birmingham Hippodrome and co-runs a workshop at Birmingham Buddhist Centre. His poems have previously appeared in *Magma*, *Under The Radar*, and on BBC Radio 4.

Julie Hogg is a poet from the North Yorkshire coast. Her debut pamphlet is *Majuba Road* (Vane Women Press, 2016). Her poems have appeared in magazines including *Butcher's Dog*, *Honest Ulsterman*, and *Popshot*. She reviews for London Grip and is writing the final touches to her first full collection.

Amanda Holiday lives in South London with her teenage daughter. She completed the Poetry MA at UEA with Distinction in 2019. Her poems have appeared in *Critical Fish*, *Prairie Schooner*, and *South Bank Poetry*. She is currently shortlisted for The Brunel International African Poetry Prize 2020.

Safiya Kamaria Kinshasa is a British-born Barbadian-raised poet and dancer. She has been commissioned by The Original Wailers and BBC Bitesize. Her poems have appeared in journals including *The Caribbean Writer*, *Finished Creatures*, and *The Amistad*. Her work is also published in *Alter Egos* (Bad Betty Press, 2019).

Anna Lawrence lives near Birmingham with her partner, four children, and a dog. She is author of *Ruby's Spoon* (Chatto & Windus, 2010). Her poems have appeared in *Bare Fiction* and she is currently working on a collection of prose and poetry drawing on her interest in women's enclosure and escape.

Philip Miller is a writer and journalist based in Edinburgh. He is the author of two novels *The Blue Horse* (Freight Books, 2015) and *All The Galaxies* (Freight Books, 2017). He was announced as a Robert Louis Stevenson Fellow in 2019. He has recently completed a new novel.

Jenny Mitchell's debut collection *Her Lost Language* (Indigo Dreams Publishing, 2019) was Poetry Kit Book of the Month. She was joint-winner of the annual Geoff Stevens' Memorial Poetry Prize 2019. Her work has appeared in magazines including *The Rialto*, *The New European*, and *The Interpreter's House*.

Jessica Mookherjee is of Bengali heritage and grew up in Swansea. She has been widely published in magazines, including *Under the Radar*, *The North*, and *Rialto*. She was highly commended in the Forward Prizes 2017 for Best Single Poem. Her second collection is *Tigress* (Nine Arches Press, 2019).

J. L. M. Morton lives in Gloucestershire. She is Poet in Residence at Waterland (Lake 32, Cotswold Water Park) and has recently had poems published widely, including by Yew Tree Press, Black Eyes Publishing, and in *Atrium*. She placed second in the 2019 Stroud Book Festival Poetry Competition.

S. Niroshini is a writer and poet based in London. Her work has appeared in publications such as *The Good Journal*, *On Bodies: An Anthology* (3 of Cups Press, 2018), and *harana poetry*. She was recently awarded a London Writers Award for Literary Fiction.

Richard O'Brien is a poet, playwright and lecturer based in Birmingham, where he is currently the city's Poet Laureate. His most recent pamphlet is *A Bloody Mess* (Valley Press, 2020). His poems have appeared in *The Poetry Review*, *Subtropics*, and *The White Review*. He won an Eric Gregory Award in 2017.

Lotte Mitchell Reford is a London-based poet and editor who holds an MLitt in Creative Writing from the University of Glasgow. Her poems have appeared in magazines including *Hobart*, *Crabfat*, and *Lighthouse*.

Matt Riker lives in the city of Biel, Switzerland. His poems have appeared in various anthologies and journals, among them *Oxford Poetry*, *Acumen,* and *Neon*.

Anna Robinson is from London. She has had two collections from Enitharmon Press and her next collection, *Whatsname Street*, is due from Smokestack in 2021. Her poems have appeared in *Poetry London*, *Oxford Poetry*, and *Long Poem Magazine*.

Marli Roode lives in Manchester. Her debut novel, *Call It Dog* (Atlantic, 2013), was shortlisted for the Dylan Thomas Prize, longlisted for the Sunday Times Fiction Prize, and was a finalist for the K. Sello Duiker Memorial Literary Award. Her ecopoetry was longlisted for the 2019 Gingko Prize.

Robert Selby has had poems and reviews appear in publications including *PN Review*, *Poetry London*, and *The Times Literary Supplement*. His debut pamphlet was published in 2017, in the Clutag Five Poems series and his debut collection, *The Coming-Down Time*, is newly published by Shoestring Press.

Kate Elspeth Simpson is an editor, journalist, and poet based in York. She edits *Aesthetica Magazine* and works across a number of its events and awards including the Aesthetica Art Prize, Creative Writing Award and Future Now Symposium. She reads for *Frontier Poetry* and has also written for *The London Magazine*, *Mslexia*, and Poetry School.

Jon Stone was born and lives in Derbyshire. He won an Eric Gregory Award in 2012, the Poetry London Prize in 2014 and 2016, and the Live Canon International Poetry Prize in 2018. He has recently completed a doctorate in poem-game hybrids.

Ellora Sutton lives in rural Hampshire. She was commended in the 2018 Winchester Poetry Prize and her debut pamphlet is forthcoming from Nightingale & Sparrow.

Ruth Taaffe is from Manchester, UK. She currently lives and works in Singapore as an English teacher. She is taking an MA in Creative Writing with Lancaster University. Her poems have been published in journals including *Nine Muses*, *Allegro,* and *Acumen*.

L. Tayba is a young poet from Sandwell. In 2016, her writing appeared in a We Are Writers anthology. She is currently working on a sequence of erasures.

Anya Trofimova is a young poet from London. She was commended in the Foyle Young Poets of the Year Award 2019. Her poems have appeared in a number of anthologies including *Planet in Peril* (Fly on the Wall Press, 2019).

Alice Willitts is a writer and plantswoman. She is the author of *Dear* (Magma, 2019) and graduated with Distinction from the Poetry MA at UEA in 2018. She was shortlisted for the Ivan Juritz Prize 2018. She leads the #57 Poetry Collective and is currently co-editing *Magma* 78 on the theme of Collaborations.

Alexa Winik is a Canadian poet and writer currently living in Edinburgh. She holds an MFA in Creative Writing from the University of St Andrews and her poetry and reviews have been published in *The Poetry Review*, *The Scores*, and *The Adroit Journal*.

Printed in Great Britain
by Amazon